Straight up entre-Hustler

Written by

John F. Hendershot

Copyright © 2021 by John F. Hendershot

All rights reserved. No part of this book may be used or reproduced by any means, graphic, electronic, or mechanical, including photocopying, recording, taping, or by any information storage retrieval system, without the written permission of the publisher except in the case of brief quotations embodied in critical articles and reviews.

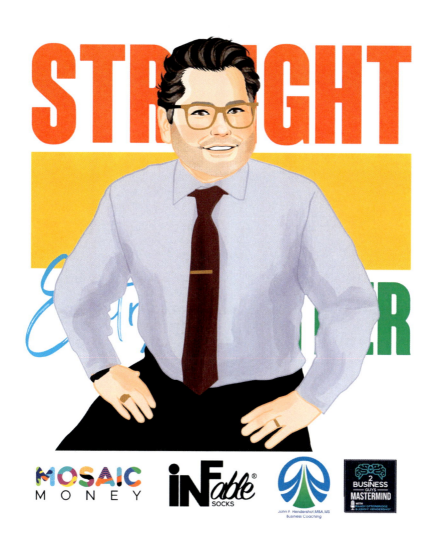

John F. Hendershot

MBA, MS Management, & BA

Experienced: Business Coach, Serial Entrepreneur, Self-Help Author, and Mentor.

January 2021

Any opinion s expressed here are those of the author and not to be considered by anyone else. All information contained herein is borne of extensive research and seasoned experience. Th e author will not take responsibility for any advice used from this book that did not end up a success. A revised version may be available directly from the author.

CONTENTS

Introduction 1

    Who is an Entre-Hustler? 4

    Entrepreneur 4

    Business Visionary 5

    What do entrepreneurs and business visionaries have in common? 5

    What is the distinction bet ween a business venture and a business? 6

Section 1: How to Go from Entrepreneur to Entre-Hustler 1

    1. Guarantee monetary strength 3

    2. Always add and hone your skills 4

    3. Recognize the issues to tackle 6

    4. Take care of this issue 7

    5. Energy to Action 8

    6. Realize when to change course 10

    7. Smart money management 12

Section 2: The Life of an Entre-Hustler: The Good, Bad, and Ugly 1

Good 2

Bad 3

Ugly 5

Section 3: Habits to Change Now if You Want to Entre-Hustle.. 6

1. Start a side hustle 7

2. Prioritize your weekends 8

3. Wake up early 9

4. Build your brand 10

5. Become an expert by adding content 11

6. Find an ally 12

7. Show restraint 13

8. Bring in cash 14

9. Network 15

11. Assess your items or potential benefits 17

12. No Glass Ceilings 18

About the Author 24

Introduction

My name is John F. Hendershot, and I was born in a small town in southcentral Ohio about an hour from the foothills of Appalahia. The town that I was raised in would be considered on the poorer-side of the American economy. Most people, my parents included, were employed as "blue-collar" workers.

As the son of the working-class poor, I watched my parents as they worked endless hours for thankless employers with both of them suffering from physical ailments due to the repetition of their so-called careers.

The truth is that my father is brilliant. As a child, he would compete on Jeopardy from our Livingroom every evening. He smoking every contestant that Alex Trebek welcomed to the show. He had a knack for reading something and being able to repeat, verbatim, what he had read years later.

We are taught as children that American's have endless opportunities. That this land which we call home is filled with milk and honey. I am not here to dispute whether American is or is not the greatest country on the planet Earth.

What I do know is that there are real barriers to opportunity that cause a lot of smart, talented, and hard-working individuals to give up before they start. Hopelessness rages through both rural communities as well as neglected urban areas.

The education that I received at Washington Court House City Schools was much different than the private school education that I am able to offer my children now. Heck, the outgoing Secretary of Education on the previous presidential cabinet received her education at the same schools as my children.

Unfortunately, I cannot see any change that a public civil servant enacts making much difference in the equation. There will always be inequities in life – it just may be presented in a different light.

The only way that I can see mitigating the perpetual system that uses us for all of our worth and spits us out when we have nothing else to offer – is through entrepreneurship; specifically, *entre-hustling.*

For the better part of the past decade, I was fortunate enough to have been introduced to entre-hustling, and the possibility of not only changing the trajectory of future generations – but to impact communities, and team members in a positive way.

I love entre-hustling, because it is a reflection of my creativity, character, and values. I love that I have the opportunity to forge change, hire people at good wages – and provide opportunities that they may have not been privy to before. I love that – a brand is not just the badge of a company but a symbol of hope, change, and opportunity.

If you have been considering starting your own business, join me as I introduce this concept of entre-hustling to you.

Who is an Entre-Hustler?

To understand *what an entre-hustler* is and if you are cut out to be one, we must first understand what is an entrepreneur.

Entrepreneur

An entrepreneur is someone that organizes and runs one or more businesses, takes greater than normal financial risks, and receives the fore most rewards.

Business Visionary

Next, we must know what is a business visionary. The business visionary is generally seen as a trailblazer, a wellspring of the most recent thoughts, item s, administrations, organizations, and cycles.

Business visionaries assume acritical role in any economy, using abilities and action to fore see needs and produce novel plans to plug. Business visionaries also figure out that in taking risks, they are compensated with benefits, notoriety, and openings for additional development.

What do entrepreneurs and business visionaries have in common?

Entrepreneurs and business visionaries know that there is always risk in their ventures, but do it anyway. Those that *don't* endure and go ahead towards success are susceptible to losing sight of their life's goals and dreams, as well as wasting away their savings.

What is the distinction bet ween a business venture and a business?

At first glance, the terms business venture and business might seem like the same thing. However, this could not be more wrong.

A *business venture* is considered an endeavor. It is when someone knowingly takes a risk in business in hopes of reaping the rewards. Not everyone is cut out to pursue business ventures. But an entre-hustler knows that in order to win big, you have to dream big and take big risks to get there.

A *business* is the result of a business venture. It's the combination of hard work, learning from past mistakes, creating a plan, relaying that plan to your employees, and executing that plan. Day in and day out, this is how a business is run.

An entre-hustler is willing to put in the risk and the work to turn a business venture into a smoothly run business.

What is a hustler?

The last term we must understand is what is a hustler.

Isn't hustling a nasty word?

Not at all.

It is common, through various time periods, cultures, and soon, for words to be hijack ed with unflattering definition s. Some might associate the term hustler with ideas of being cheap or tricking people to make their money.

However, a hustler is a forcefully venturesome individual, a hard worker. In the North

American dictionary, the primary meaning of a hustler is "an aggressively enterprising person; a go-getter." It is only by taking back the slang or jargon of a word and reclaiming and restoring it to its true definition, that we modify the space around us.

Entrepreneur + Business Visionary + Hustler= Entre-Hustler

So, what happens when a person embodies the qualities of an entrepreneur, a business visionary, and a hustler?

An Entre-Hustler is born.

Entre-Hustling is entrepreneurship+. It is a movement of people who believe that they were created to be creators.

An entre-hustler isn't just an enterprising go-getter, but also someone who strives to learn new things, as well as tries to teach others.

An entre-hustler is a leader, teacher, coach, mentor. Entre-hustlers know what it is like to have a boss that falls short of expectations and fails to inspire anything but fear in their employees. Entre-hustlers use this empathy to inform their style of leadership and create one that inspires. They go as far as providing second, even third chances to those who make mistakes, and act as a cheerleader to their employees.

Over the past 150 years, humanity has learned to "stay in school, not to create problems, and to find a good job." Entre-hustlers believe that this stays inside the lines norm that humanity has pushed suppresses creativity, dreams, and opportunities for innovation.

Entre-hustlers believe that "normal" jobs offer minimal support to their employees. You are limited when you have a regular job. Someone else controls what money you make, when you get it, and when you move up the ladder of success. But, when you choose the life of an entrepreneur, you set your limits. You can blow the roof off these limits and benefit not only yourself, but families, communities, and society as a whole.

An Entre-Hustler is a stubborn entrepreneur; an entrepreneur 10 times superior to the average entrepreneur because they will not stop, no matter how man y times they are knocked down.

It's about being your own boss, giving all you might to achieve your goals. For many people, entrepreneurship is the highest goal in terms of career.

Bu t as beautiful as it sounds, running you r business is also incredibly difficult. It's so difficult that 90% of businesses fail [Patel, Neil Forbes Magazine, January 16, 2015].

Th e good news is, star ting a business can be one of the most rewarding and exciting opportunities you 'll ever have. If you are aware of the risks and still determined to be an entrepreneur, you are on the right track.

Lucky for you, you are not alone. We are here to help. Use the strategies and tips in this guide to start your journey as an entre-hustler.

SECTION 1

How to Go from Entrepreneur to Entre-Hustler

After Judi Sheppard Missett retired and hung up her professional ballet shoes, she organized and taught a civilian dance class to make extra money. Before long, she found that the ones who came to her studio were getting in shape, improving their tone, and learning something new. Sheppard Missett then trained instructors who continued to teach their lessons to them asses, and thus Jazzercise was born. A franchise agreement soon followed, and today, the company has more than 8,900 locations around the world.

After completing a correspondence course on ice cream making, Jerry Greenfield and Ben Cohen combined the savings of $ 8,000 with a loan of t $4,000, rented a gas station in Burlington, Virginia, and introduced their unique flavors to the neighborhood market. After twenty years, Ben and Jerry's have a yearly turnover of a few million dollars.

Since the independent man / lady has arisen as a mainstream figure in American culture, the idea of starting one's own business has been romanticized over the last few decades. Many people that decide to start their own business go into it without proper preparations or expectations.

In contrast to conventional callings, which regularly have a set paths, the path from a business venture to a successful business is not set-in stone. What work s for one entre-hustler may not work for another, and vice versa.

Regardless, there are eight actions and qualities that all entre-hustlers should try to embody:

1. Guarantee monetary strength

This initial action is certainly not a severe prerequisite, yet it is suggested. While you can build a successful business without financial backing (imagine Facebook founder Mark Zuckerberg as a college student), starting with enough cash and ongoing funding can only help. Ideally, you would having enough money to expand your team and give them m or e time to build a successful business, without worrying about making money fast.

However, if you find that you don 't have enough capital to finance your first business, there is no shame in getting a paid job to help finance your dreams.

In fact, an entre-hustler does just that. They don't believe the romanticized version of starting your own business, where you have enough money starting out to put all your time and focus into the new business.

No! Entre-hustlers expect to have one or two jobs *while* building their business. They accept the overtime and odd hours they need to put in to get their business off the ground because that's what it takes. They know it will pay off in the end.

2. Always add and hone your skills

Entre-hustlers may start out with utilizing a skill they have always had. They may pursue a business in the field they received an educational degree from. For example, if a starting entre-hustler has experience in the financial sector, they might take on a sales role in their existing business to develop the inter personal skills they need to be successful.

This makes sense because when you are confident in something, you find it easier to believe you will succeed.

But entre-hustlers know that pushing your comfort zone and learning new skills will only serve to benefit their business. It's not enough to just know one thing.

It is important to expand your knowledge as your employees will look to you for knowledge and guidance. So, consume content through multiple channels:

- Take an online course
- Read books by experts
- Shadow/consult with experts
- Practice, practice, practice
- Learn from mistakes and set backs

Developing different skills is just as important as the need to consume different content. An entre-hustler is always informed on the current information available about their industry. Stay informed. Consume content through:

- Digital recordings
- Books
- Articles
- Public gatherings
- Newsletters

3. Recognize the issues to tackle

By staying informed in your industry and increasing your skill set, you will put yourself in a better position to add value to your customer's lives.

You will be able to identify what issues or concerns customers want help solving. Then, you can position your business as the lead business in solving that problem.

Think of it this way; you never want customers to consider your business as obsolete. You must be willing and able to pivot and adapt your business to meet customer needs.

An entre-hustler expects this and prepares for it.

4. Take care of this issue

After identifying an issue or concern to tackle, an entre-hustler wastes no time in making a plan. They work with their employees to map out the steps. They use their wealth of knowledge accumulated from Action 3, to inform their planning.

Unlike the average entrepreneur who might want to take the reigns on a project and be in control, an entre-hustler gets input from their employees.

They know that they hired these employees for a reason and that their knowledge and skills are useful. If they weren't, what would be the point in hiring them?

By listening to their employees, entre-hustlers promote a positive working environment where people feel trusted by their boss; therefore, producing a higher volume if quality work.

5. Energy to Action

Entre-hustlers know how to turn energy into action. Their goal is to inspire those around them, to pass on the hardworking energy that fuels them every day to their employees.

Entre-hustlers know that the best work comes from those that are happy and energized about what they are doing. That's why they hire others who are energetically fired up about what they are doing.

Then, entre-hustlers takes that energy and apply it to the plans they made in Actions 3 and 4. They turn their plans into reality with the help of their team, who is just as energized due to the healthy work environment their leader has created.

Entre-hustlers aren't afraid to get their hands dirty

The attitude and spirit of the entre-hustler, especially at the initial stage, is important.

The entre-hustler is not afraid to get their hands dirty. Whether that means putting in extra hours or managing clients one on one, by themselves, at the beginning.

Besides, it is important to, whenever possible, per son ally m an age sales and other inter act ion s with customers. Direct contact with clients in the beginning is the most straight forward approach to get fair criticism on what your intended interest group likes and what you could improve.

In addition, the entre-hustler knows that great first impression as that create a personal relationship with clients is the key to gaining more clients. One happy client could be the key to hundreds more through word of mouth and positive reviews.

Entre-hustlers know the value of being accessible to their customers. For example, a carport startup with a preferable site can attract more clients compared to a $100 million carport business without a website.

One of the top ways to please a customer is to always be accessible. When starting out, entre-hustlers will need a phone, an email and a website.

Simply ensuring there's a live individual on the opposite end of the telephone, email or website help center can make all the difference.

6. Realize when to change course

Former Starbucks President and CEO, Howard Schultz, originally believed that playing Italian opera music through the store's speakers would add to the Italian coffee experience he was trying to replicate. However, clients saw it diversely and didn't appear to like their coffee tunes. Accordingly, Schultz jettisoned the drama house and presented com for table seats, all things considered.

Hardly any business gets it right the first time around.

Just as a chef doesn't expect a recipe to be right the first time cooking it, an entre-hustler is prepared to switch up their recipe for success.

Entre-hustlers expect change due to strategies not working, the ever-changing market, and inevitable changes in their industry.

Instead of trying to fight it, entre-hustlers embrace the need for change. That is what they prepare for through their content consumption and learning new skills.

7. Smart money management

Action 2 stated that entre-hustlers are always learning new skills to aid in the success of their business. One of those skills must be money management.

At the heart of a successful new business is a stable cash flow needed to buy inventory, pay rent, maintain equipment, and run the business. Keeping track of income and expenses is the key to staying in the black.

Entre-hustlers know that most new businesses don't make a profit in the first year. That is why they are prepared to allocate funds to their business with a second job to reduce the risk of running out of funds.

With that in mind, it's important to keep personal and business expenses separate and never invest in business funds to cover day-to-day expenses.

Obviously, when the business is making a profit, it's imperative to pay yourself a genuine compensation that will cover the minimum necessities.

Questions to Consider Before Pursuing the life of an Entre-Hustler

Beginning an innovative profession and becoming your own boss is can be one of the most rewarding experiences.

But make sure to consider these questions before getting started.

A few inquiries to pose

- Do I have the character, the disposition, and the mindset to assume control over the world on my standing?
- Do I have the correct air and the correct assets to commit the entirety of my chance to my business?

- Do I have a prepared exit plan with very much characterized timetables in case of my business failing?

- Do I have a particular arrangement for the following "x" months, or will I have issues in route because of family, monetary or different responsibilities? Do I have an arrangement to lighten these issues?

- Am I all around associated with request help and counsel when required? [i.e., Legal/ Accounting].

- Have I recognized and developed ranges with experienced mentors to acquire from their experiences?

- Have I arranged a full dan ger appraisal [SWOT analysis], including outside designs?

- Have I practically evaluated the capability of my proposition and how it might be reflect ed in the current market?

- If my offer replaces a current item available, how might my rivals respond?

- Does it bode well to get a patent to secure my proposition? Would I be able endure the process and wait time?

- Did I at first characterize my ideal clients? Do I have extension plan s for bigger business sectors?

- Have I recognized the types of business deals and appropriation channels?

Questions about external factors:

- Does my business comply with local codes and regulations? Since it is beyond the realm of imagination locally, can I and would it be advisable for me to move to another area?

- How long does it take to obtain the necessary license or authorizations from the competent authorities? Can I survive that long?

- Do I have a plan to secure the necessary resources, qualified personnel, and have I fact or ed in the costs?

- What is the assessed time span for putting a model available for different administrations?

- Who are my guideline clients?

- What wellsprings of financing would it be advisable for me to go to be fruitful? Is a decent arrangement enough to persuade expect ed partners?

- What specialized framework do I need?

- When the business is set up, will I have enough assets to take the business to the next level? Are other large organizations going to duplicate my model and crush my work?

SECTION 2

The Life of an Entre-Hustler: The Good, Bad, and Ugly

Entre-hustling is a way of life. Entre-hustlers are prepared to work hard and never give up.

Unfortunately, many people are motivated by money when starting a business venture. An entre-hustler, though their goal is ultimately to earn a profit, is motivated by taking what they are passionate about and turning it into a business.

Entre-hustlers are motivated by the value they add to their client/customer's lives. Entre-hustlers are problem-solvers.

If you are unsure whether to be an entre-hustler, here is the good, bad, and ugy about being your own boss.

Good

It is understood that owning your own business can be rewarding in many ways:

- Financial freedom
- Control over decisions
- Control over who you hire
- Control over the hours you work

When you take on the qualities of an entre-hustler, your are rewarded in many more ways:

- Trust and respect from employees that feel valued and heard
- Employees are motivated to give 110% due to your positive leadership that comes from a place of understanding and empathy.

- Daily inspiration to improve your business due to the inspirational people you surround yourself with and the content influx of knowledge you are consuming about your industry.
- Financial freedom that allows you to give back to your community.
- Genuine connections with client/customers due to establishing yourself as a leader, a mentor, and a person of honor.

Bad

There is no magic formula that brings instant success and wealth. The life of an entre-hustler, though completely doable, may not be for everyone. So, it is important to understand the downsides of starting your own business as an entre-hustler. Can you handle these:

- Most new business do not turn a profit in their first year. Entre-hustlers are prepared to have a second or third job while getting their business off the ground.

- Monthly income fluctuates depending on how the business is doing and the economy. Entre-hustlers save and spend wisely. They do not prevent themselves from enjoying life, but know how to live within their means.

- Nothing is certain. Stress can happen. Entre-hustlers are prepared to put in the work to minimize the amount of unknowns in their business. They also have self care routines in place to manage stress.

- Entre-hustlers have people, family and employees, relying on them financially. The state of their business can often affect their relationships. Entre-hustlers are prepared to speak openly with their family and employees to set realistic expectations and boundaries.

Ugly

Truthfully, there is no ugly unless you make it. You are responsible for how your business is managed. Sure, you can't control the economy and there are things out of your control, but the ugly only shows up in your business if you create it.

To prevent the ugly, do the following:

- Research and follow the laws that revolve around your business.
- Keep proper documentation: contracts, finances, and communication.
- Keep on building your skills.
- Keep on expanding your knowledge.
- Stay in touch with your audience's wants and needs. Use it to inform your business moves.

SECTION 3

Habits to Change Now if You Want to Entre-Hustle

If you're in your early 20s and 30s, you are lucky enough to be living through a generational shift in power.

Generations Y and Z have incredible opportunities. While your parents' generation had to spend time working to climb the corporate ladder, you have a faster (and more fun) alternative. As you grow with technology, you gain a competitive advantage to build brands that rely on digital marketing and technology.

If you want to start the next Facebook or Twitter, open a marketing agency or become an

Instagram influencer, it's time to stop chasing other people's lives on social media and start working on your business.

As your friends take advantage of the Sunday Fun day and go out on Thursday nights, you can expand your business and lay the foundation for your future success.

Below are some ways to get started being your own boss as a entre-hustler and habits to begin forming to ensure success.

1. Start a side hustle

Most people under estimate just how many hours of their life they use at work when in a 9 to 5 job. For something to take up that much time in your life, you better love it. If you have found that you don't like your job, stop complaining and take action.

Start a side. Side hustles are a great way to get started creating a business. Whether its to start making the extra money needed to finance your business, or to do a cold open of the type of business you want to scale later, getting started is the first step.

So, have a cup of coffee after work and start work at 18:00, and at 2 am in your new venture.

If you are an artist, start posting a video on YouTube about the details of the design process.

Try to build up your business by operating an e-commerce store on Shopify. Build up your market with promotions on Instagram. All of this can be done in parallel to expanding your business. Best of all, you still get someone else's salary.

2. Prioritize your weekends

If you are truly passionate about being an entre-hustler, you will quickly discover that the weekend is the most productive time to work. You can dedicate 20 hours of work over the weekend to grow your brand without giving up precious self-care time.

But this will not happen if you go to bars on Friday and Saturday nights for the sake of an Instagram photo. Ultimately, you will waste money and time that could be better spent growing your business.

So, start setting your alarm for 6:30 am on weekends. You won't regret losing a nigh t or two when you're in your 30s, running a million-dollar business and making your own schedule.

3. Wake up early

Apple CEO, Tim Cook, is known for waking up early and sending emails to the company at 4:30 a.m. The youngest NBA CEO, Brett Jormark, gets up at 3:30 and arrives at the office at 4:30.

With regards to business, whoever wants it most will win in the end. Entre-hustlers have an offensive mindset. Instead of let ting things happen, they are deliberate about getting a daily head start.

Bonus Tip: Make sure to set an alar m on the opposite side of the room so that you get out of bed and don't press the snooze button. Do 50 push-ups within 5 minutes after turning off the alarm to wake up.

4. Build your brand

I'm often surprised at how much businesses spend on social media to promote themselves, but then don't have a website to match this level of promotion. Their websites lacks information, lacks branding and fails to provide ways to stay in contact with customers.

A few things to consider when branding your business:

- What is my company's value to my customers?

- What message does my company represent?
- Does my company name and website reflect what my business does/is?
- Do I have a logo and brand colors? Are they present on my website, social media, and products?

Bonus Tip: Everyone should see if their first and last names are available for purchase on Go Daddy. If you have a common name, enter your middle name and profession as part of the URL (for example, SarahSmithNYCArtist.com). Th e next time you go to a business meeting, you will be surprised to see how people are impressed with your professional website.

5. Become an expert by adding content

In addition to a business coach, I am also a partner on the e-commerce stock website. We just started a sportswear business and launched a website called Mosaic Money [www.mosaic-money.com]. My business is always growing because that is what an entre-hustler does.

An entre-hustler is always adding content for their customers to enjoy. Whether it be a new product or a new article/blog to their website, entre-hustlers do not let things get stale.

6. Find an ally

When you are an entrepreneur, you live on an isolated island. Nobody will see how hard you work every day. Your friends, who work from 9 am to 5 pm daily, will know what your company means to you but they might not be able to completely relate with you.

Since entrepreneurship can be lonely, make sure you have someone to talk to about it.

Whether your spouse, girlfriend, boyfriend, mom, dad, or just a mentor you can trust, find someone that can be an ally.

7. Show restraint

The issue with the computerized age we live in now is that individuals have become rest less. Restlessness in business can be dangerous. Rushed plans can result in outcomes that don't pan out because of a lack of intentionality and planning.

Bill Gates referred to the acclaimed articulation, "By far most over estimate what they can do in one year and deride what they can do in ten years."

To begin a business, you must show restraint in the long haul. Entre-hustlers know how to make a plan and when to stick with it or adapt it for the best results.

Decide where you want your business to be in a year; think about your goals for the next 10 years and how you will achieve them to make all of your ambitions come true.

Ensure you complete things rapidly yet show restraint for long haul results.

I have had my business for practically ten years.

I know 96% of organizations come up short before the age of 10 [Wilde, Heather. Inc Magazine. August 02, 2018]. I remember this measurement consistently on the grounds that I need to be essential for the 4 percent of this seriousness.

8. Bring in cash

Entre- hustlers don't just dream. They act on their dreams. On the off chance that you are not bringing in cash with your business, you need to begin, and you need to begin soon. All the same, as a hockey group needs to score to dominate a match, your business needs to bring in cash to be a business. Qu it imagining and begin selling an item or administration.

9. Network

Begin connecting with other entre-hsutlers in your industry from around the world. You will likewise be propelled and encouraged by connecting with somebody who is effective and creating change in your industry.

Don 't think for a second that you're the only one benefiting from widening your circle - the CEOs and founders you meet, who are probably in their 40s, 50s, and 60s, will ask you a lot of questions. Why? Customers are likely your age and understand the buying power of Gen Y and Gen Z. CEOs will want to know your secrets to success as much as you want to know theirs.

10. Become a SEO master and pay to promote

Entre-hustlers search for a superior method to develop your business. Establishing visibility to your client base is a start.

Get yourself on the first page of Google so that individuals can get in touch with you easily for business opportunities. Whet her you're a graduate and wanting to begin your training or sell custom accessories, SEO and web-based promoting can help any business.

Entre-hustlers know that they do not need an advanced education or a class to be a SEO or PPC master. You simply have to be willing to get your hands grimy.

- Read books on SEO
- Read articles
- Watch videos
- Find free workshops with experts
- Do an SEO audit, or hire someone to do it for you.

When first starting out, you should have a basic comfort level so that you can create leads and deals online consistently.

11. Assess your items or potential benefits

Entre-hustlers know how to budget. And if they don't know, they make it a priority to learn how. Set forth a fearless exertion to put aside money. No one can really tell when the economy will go down or when your top client/customer will drop out. Overspending will leave you in the trenches when a financial curve ball in thrown your way. And, trust me, those curve balls will happen no matter how your business is run.

So, if you are just starting out, begin saving money by eating more peanut butter and jelly sandwiches. Eat out less.

Stop buying pieces of clothing at Nordstrom and start shopping at TJ Maxx. Incidentally, when you go into TJ Maxx or Marsh all's stores, check out my sock brand iNFable.

Every piece of income is important when you are setting up a business. Warren Buffett has lived in the very same house in Omaha, Nebraska, that he purchased for $58,000 in 1958. The genuine victors in business are brilliant with their cash.

12. No Glass Ceilings

Entre-hustlers enjoy using their inventiveness and abilities to create abundance for their communities, their families, and themselves.

There is always a ceiling when you have a job in which you are not the boss. Entre-hustlers can break through that ceiling and benefit society as a whole, families, communities, and themselves.

Entre-hustlers also know that there is no ceiling when it comes to growing their business.

To grow and prosper, most businesses must continually improve their products and services through continuous innovation and necessary changes. Products and services wear out, become obsolete, and are no longer competitive. To survive, companies must also create new products and services to satisfy unmet needs.

Businesses that rely solely on innovation will thrive.

Entre-hustlers are more likely to be actively creating and innovating all the time. They are strategic with their priorities, allowing them an advantage in business over their competition.

Entre-hustlers see innovation as a source of success in a market economy, an opinion reinforced by the evolution of today's competitive environment.

Today, we're in a society where competition forces companies to be great and operate with integrity and social awareness. Customers expect businesses to always be improving their products.

A business that is neither imaginative nor inventive can't make do in today's market.

Advancement is all about considering every fact or that will help improve your business to gain the upper hand in the market. Inventiveness and development are at the core of a business venture.

Quotes by John F. Hendershot

- Organizational strength lies in the ability to surround ourselves with radically different perspectives without feeling threatened.
- One of the biggest mistakes that a businessperson can make is to underestimate the need and value to continuously build their network.

- You were created for so much more than you can imagine.
- You are worth it! Believe.
- Leader ship is more about yielding than wielding power.
- Leaders, entrepreneurs, as well as any good citizen should not be satisfied with just getting through life - because when we are entrusted with anyone, they are entrusting us with their lives, therefore they deserve to be influenced by someone that does not wield aim less power but strives to empower those around them.
- You matter.
- I believe that at the core of every person there is a desire to radiate goodness and Love.
- I believe that life is much bigger than myself, and I want to positively impact our world.

- Leadership is a state of mind. It means that you believe in something so idealistically - that you know that you can help make a difference.
- Be who you were created to be.
- Sometimes we get too caught up in the chase, that we miss the most important aspects of life.
- If God loves us unconditionally - doesn't that mean, we are obligated to do the same - to everyone?
- Finding a solution to the problem instead of giving up is success.
- Managers or co-workers that belittle their team member are in turn exposing their own insecurities.
- Blowing out someone else's candle is not going to cause yours to shine through.
- Money is a tool in the same way that a hammer is a tool. Just because you have

the best hammer doesn't make you a master craftsman. It is the quality of the person utilizing the tool that allows each tool to work effectively to complete the task.

- There is a better way to conduct business - a better way to partner and treat people.
- Attitude, not title, is the key indicator of leadership.
- Leadership is about responsibility, not power.
- I would rather feel discomfort, than to die rich, but refuse to look out for those that walked beside me.

About the Author

My name is John F. Hendershot, and I was born in a small town in southcentral Ohio about an hour from the foothills of Appalachia. The town that I was raised in would be considered on the poorer-side of the American economy. Most people, my parents included, were employed as "blue-collar" workers.

As the son of the working-class poor, I watched my parents as they worked endless hours for thankless employers, both of them suffering from physical ailments due to the repetition of their so-called careers.

The truth is that my father is brilliant. As a child, he would compete on Jeopardy from our living room every evening, smoking every contestant that Alex Trebek welcomed to the show. He had a knack for reading something and being able to repeat, verbatim, what he had read years later.

We are taught as children that American's have endless opportunities. That this land which we call home is filled with milk and honey. I am not here to dispute whether American is or is not the greatest country on the planet Earth.

What I do know is that there are real barriers to opportunity that cause a lot of smart, talented, and hard-working individuals to give up before they start. Hopelessness rages through both rural communities as well as neglected urban areas.

The education that I received at Washington Court House City Schools was much different than the private school education that I am able to offer my children now. Heck, the outgoing Secretary of Education on the previous presidential cabinet received her education at the same schools as my children.

Unfortunately, I cannot see any change that a public civil servant enacts making much difference in the equation. There will always be inequities in life – it just may be presented in a different light.

The only way that I can see mitigating the perpetual system that uses us for all of our worth and spits us out when we have nothing else to offer – is through entrepreneurship; specifically, entre-hustling.

For the better part of the past decade, I was fortunate enough to have been introduced to entre-hustling, and the possibility of not only changing the trajectory of future generations – but to impact communities, and team members in a positive way.

I love entre-hustling because it is a reflection of my creativity, character, and values. I love that I have the opportunity to forge change, hire people at good wages – and provide opportunities that they may have not been privy to before. I love that – a brand is not just the badge of a company but a symbol of hope, change, and opportunity.

Made in the USA
Columbia, SC
07 March 2021